# THOUGHTS OF OG MANDINO

by craig lock

*"Success is not to be pursued.*
*It is attracted by the person you become."*

*"I will love the light for it shows me the way, yet I will endure the darkness because it shows me the stars."*
- Og Mandino

Just sharing some uplifting thoughts by Og Mandino
Perhaps the most widely read self help author in the world!
Just Sharing Some Thoughts from my blog
www.ogmandinobooks.wordpress.com

Tags (key words): inspiration, Og Mandino, Og Mandino books, inspirational thoughts, faith, hope, love

THOUGHTS OF OG MANDINO: on HOPE, FAITH, DREAMS, PEACE and all through the Power of Love

enjoy

Submitter's Note:

I feel that this powerful message is so vital for all people in the world to hear and it's great that Og Mandino's generous spirit lives on through these words. In this e-book In some small way I'm trying to spread the message ... as well as "carrying a torch" helping keep Og's great legacy and messages of hope alive for future generations.

craig

"We share what we know, so that we all may grow."

"From the depth of the valleys, in the deserts of despair, there is hope... as there is the unquenchable oasis, the immense breadth and depth of the human spirit... always."

"When (or is it perhaps if??) you arrive in a place (or rather state ) known as heaven, let faith, hope and love be the wings of the chariot that carried you there."

-craig (as adapted from the words of Jonathan Edwards, a former minister in Massachusetts (New England)

"Together, one mind, one soul, one life at a time (with God's help), let's see how many people we can impact, empower, encourage and perhaps even inspire to reach their fullest potentials.

"When hope endures, dreams persist ... and never die."

- craig

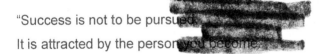

"Success is not to be pursued.
It is attracted by the person you become."

*"I will love the light for it shows me the way, yet I will endure the*

*darkness because it shows me the stars."*

*- Og Mandino*

http://www.ogmandino.com

http://www.ogmandino.com/ogmandino_for_the_21st_century

# 

A Better Way to Live

by Og Mandino,

The author recounts his descent into despair and his discovery of spiritual nourishment in the works of Aristotle, Emerson, Ben Franklin, and Plato, and enumerates the seventeen rules that helped transform his life.

His rules in this book are rules for a better way to live. They include:

1) Count your blessings.

2) Deliver more than what you are getting paid to do.

3) Do not dwell on your past mistakes.

4) Surround yourself with your family especially if you spend long hours away from them.

5) Build this day on a foundation of pleasant thoughts.

6) Let your action speak louder than your words. But be careful of conceit and pride.

7) Look at each day as a gift from God.

8) Do not spend your days on unnecessary clutter but on productive tasks.

9) Live each day as though it was your last.

10) Treat everyone you know or meet as though you will be dead by midnight.

11) Laugh at yourself and at life.

12) Never neglect the little things.

13) Welcome every morning with a smile.

14) Set your goals on a daily basis.

15) Never allow anyone or anything to rain on your parade.

16) Search for the seed of good in every adversity.

17) Realize that true happiness lies within you.

He expands on each of his rules. Og Mandino portrays that the time we have on earth is limited. We should make the most of each and every minute in order to live a better way of live.

"A Better Way to Live" is one of those books that reaches out to the reader in all of us--a book that is designed by its author, Og Mandino, to inspire and uplift, motivate and and captivate us into overcoming everyday difficulties and...

"Choice! The key is choice. You have options. You need not spend your life wallowing in failure, ignorance, grief, poverty, shame and self-pity! There is always a better way to live!"

Make it Count

"Success is not to be pursued.

It is attracted by the person you become."

"I will love the light for it shows me the way, yet I will endure the darkness because it shows me the stars."

- Og Mandino

From my blog

www.ogmandinobooks.wordpress.com

enjoy

*

"Beginning today, treat everyone you meet as if they were going to be dead by midnight. Extend to them all the care, kindness and understanding you can muster, and do so with no thought of any reward. Your life will never be the same again."

"Beginning today, treat everyone you meet as if they were going to be dead by midnight. Extend to them all the care, kindness, and understanding you can muster, and do it with no thought of any reward. Your life will never be the same again."

Og Mandino

happytoin

*"Beginning today, treat everyone you meet as if they were going to be dead by midnight. Extend to them all the **care, kindness** and **understanding** you can muster, and do so **with no thought of any reward. Your life will never be the same again.**"*
— Og Mandino


**"Together, one heart, one mind, one life, one small step at a time, let's plant the seeds of a better and brighter future."**
PPS
Best wishes from the First City to see the light each new day

Picture (great) by my friend, Jenny, whose photographic talents I definitely do NOT possess!
from
www.jennysphotographicjourney.wordpress.com
www.onetaleoftwocities.wordpress.com
www.itsalwaysdarkestbeforethedawn.wordpress.com
www.shatteredbrokendreams.wordpress.com
www.lifeisgodsnovel.wordpress.com

# THE GREATEST MIRACLE IN THE WORLD

by Og Mandino

A magnificent obsession

Here are some of my notes (brief) from this "heart-warming" and uplifting book, that I read some years back

Enjoy…

*"Also I heard the voice of the Lord saying, 'Whom shall I send, and who will go for us?' Then said I, 'Here am I; send me'."*
Isaiah 6:8
*"Now go, write it before them in a table and note it in a book, that it may be for the time to come for ever and ever."*
Isaiah 30:8
1. **Count your blessings**
2. **Proclaim your rarity**
3. **Go another** (the extra) **mile** for others
4. **The power of choice** in our lives
5. **Do all things with love**.
These simple rules will help you perform, achieve a miracle in your own life.

The great miracle in the world is YOU!

*"Every noble work at first seems impossible."*
– Thomas Carlyle
and

*"It always seems impossible…*
*until it gets done."*
–Nelson Mandela
from http://www.mandelamadiba.wordpress.com

Thoreau's axiom: *"Men were born to **succeed**, not fail."*
Stirling Moss's (my boyhood hero) famous quote: "I was
taught that everything is attainable, if you're prepared to
give up, to sacrifice to get it. Whatever you ant to do, you
can do it, if you want to do it badly enough…. and I do
believe that."
pg 54
A shining example of how much it was possible to
accomplish with ones life, despite obstacles and handicaps
*"This world has provided me with everything a man could*
*desire. It is time I began to repay my debt by doing all I*
*can to make a better life for all mankind.*
YOU can light one tiny light in the darkness

# The greatest miracle in the world is **YOU!**

*

*You are the greatest miracle in the world*

*"Consider a painting by Rembrandt or a bronze by Degas or a violin by Stradivarius or a play by Shakespeare. They have great value for two reasons: their creators were masters and they are few in number. Yet there are more than one of each of these.*

*On that reasoning you are the most valuable treasure on the face of the earth, for you know who created you and there is only one of you.*

*Never, in all of the seventy billion humans who have walked this planet since the beginning of time has there been anyone exactly like you.*

*Never, until the end of time, will there be another such as you.*

*You have shown no knowledge or appreciation of your uniqueness.*

*Yet, you are the rarest thing in the world."*

— *Og Mandino, The Greatest Miracle in World*

from

https://yourhappyplaceblog.com/2014/02/21/lessons-learned-from-the-movie-winters-tale-og-mandino/

\*

THE GREATEST SALESMAN IN THE WORLD (Part Two)

The End of the Story

in his books Og Mandino has distilled the wisdom of the ages.

"For it is written, I will destroy the wisdom of the wise, and will bring to nothing the understanding of the prudent. What have they, the philosopher, the writer, and the critic of this world to show for all their wisdom? Has not God made the wisdom of this world look foolish?"

1 Corinthians 1:19-20

We all have the power to pray- light (up) the lamp of **faith**
*"**Prayer** is the **key** that opens the door to God's blessing."*
Be enthusiastic
*"The creation of a thousand forests is in a single acorn."*
– Ralph Waldo Emerson

*"From tiny acorns giant oak-trees grow."*

"Together, one mind, one life (one small step at a time), let's see how many people (and lives) we can encourage, impact, empower, enrich, uplift and perhaps even inspire to reach their fullest potentials…and strive for and perhaps one sunny day even achieve their wildest dreams."
PPS

Best wishes from the First City to see the light each new day

Picture (great) by my friend, Jenny, whose photographic talents I definitely do NOT possess!
from
www.jennysphotographicjourney.wordpress.com
www.onetaleoftwocities.wordpress.com
www.itsalwaysdarkestbeforethedawn.wordpress.com
www.shatteredbrokendreams.wordpress.com
www.lifeisgodsnovel.wordpress.com
www.climbingmountainsandchasingdreams.wordpress.co
m
and
www.awritersdreams.wordpress.com

**THE CHOICE (by Og Mandino)**

1

!

Here are some of my notes from this heart-warming and uplifting book.

Enjoy

THERE IS A BETTER WAY TO LIVE.

A book to kindle the flame of hope in every reader

How to Conquer Life

A Better Way of Living

How to get anything you want in life.

*"Death is not a foe, but an invisible adventure."*

and

*"Death is the golden key that opens the palace of eternity."* (pg 156)

"My achievements will never rise higher than my faith in myself.

– Og Mandino

"We've given that special ingredient many names over the years- **soul, spirit, light, flame;** but what we call it is not important, so long as we realize that we have it – **a special gift, a gift from God**. The trouble is that this mysterious force, whatever name you hang on it, is dormant in the majority of humans, usually through no fault of their own." (pg 111)

The image you hold of yourself is key.

There is a better way to live…

and you have discovered the missing key.

Choose to use it!

from

"Together, one mind, one life (one small step at a time), let's see how many people (and lives) we can encourage, impact, empower, enrich, uplift and perhaps even inspire to reach their fullest potentials."
PPS
*"I will love the light for it shows me the way, yet I will endure the darkness because it shows me the stars."*
– Og Mandino

Pictures (great) by my friend, Jenny, whose photographic talents I definitely do NOT possess!
from
www.jennysphotographicjourney.wordpress.com
www.onetaleoftwocities.wordpress.com
www.itsalwaysdarkestbeforethedawn.wordpress.com
www.shatteredbrokendreams.wordpress.com
www.lifeisgodsnovel.wordpress.com
www.climbingmountainsandchasingdreams.wordpress.com
and
www.awritersdreams.wordpress.com

Best wishes from the First City to see the light each new day
PPS

**DON'T use Windows 10 with WordPress** (it's driving me flipp'n crazy trying to edit submissions)!
THE CHOICE!

Posted in Uncategorized | 1 ReplyEdit
**"Failure will never overtake me, if my determination to succeed is strong enough."**
Posted on **June 5, 2016**
4

FAILURE WIL
NEVER OVERTAK
ME IF M
DETERMINATIO
TO SUCCEED I
STRONG ENOUGH

OG MANDII

from http://www.youcanbeachampion.wordpress.com

"Together, one mind, one life (one small step at a time), let's see how many people (and lives) we can encourage, impact, empower, enrich, uplift and perhaps even inspire to reach their fullest potentials…and strive for and perhaps one sunny day even achieve their wildest dreams."

pictures from

Appendix

For more of Craig's books on Og Mandino see

https://www.amazon.com/Thoughts-Og-Mandino-darkness-Champion-ebook/

https://www.amazon.com/Thoughts-Og-Mandino-Better-Live/dp/1490503463

and

https://www.amazon.com/s/ref=nb_sb_noss?url=search-alias%3Daps&field-keywords=craig+lock+%2B+og+Mandino

"Together, one mind, one life (one small step at a time), let's see how many people (and lives) we can encourage, impact, empower, enrich, uplift and perhaps even inspire to reach their fullest potentials...and strive for and perhaps one sunny day even achieve their wildest dreams."

The various books* that Craig "felt inspired to write" are available at http://www.amazon.com/-/e/B005GGMAW4
http://www.amazon.com/s/ref=la_B005GGMAW4_sr?rh=i%3Abooks&field-author=Craig+Lock
https://www.createspace.com/pub/simplesitesearch.search.do?sitesearch_query=%22craig+lock%22&sitesearch_type=STORE
http://www.creativekiwis.com/index.php/books
and http://goo.gl/vTpjk
All proceeds go to needy and underprivileged children –

MINE!

"When the writer is no more , the value of your purchase will soar! "

"Together, one mind, one life (one small step at a time), let's see how many people (and lives) we can encourage, impact, empower, enrich, uplift and perhaps even inspire to reach their fullest potentials...and strive for and perhaps one sunny day even achieve their wildest dreams."

PPS

Don't worry about the world ending today...

as it's already tomorrow in scenic and tranquil 'little' New Zealand

Picture (great) by my friend, Jenny, whose photographic talents I definitely do NOT possess!

from

www.jennysphotographicjourney.wordpress.com

www.onetaleoftwocities.wordpress.com

www.itsalwaysdarkestbeforethedawn.wordpress.com

www.shatteredbrokendreams.wordpress.com

www.lifeisgodsnovel.wordpress.com

www.climbingmountainsandchasingdreams.wordpress.com

and

www.awritersdreams.wordpress.com

THE END (for now)

*************************

CPSIA information can be obtained
at www.ICGtesting.com
Printed in the USA
LVOW13s0009230317

528173LV00008B/141/P